D1716802

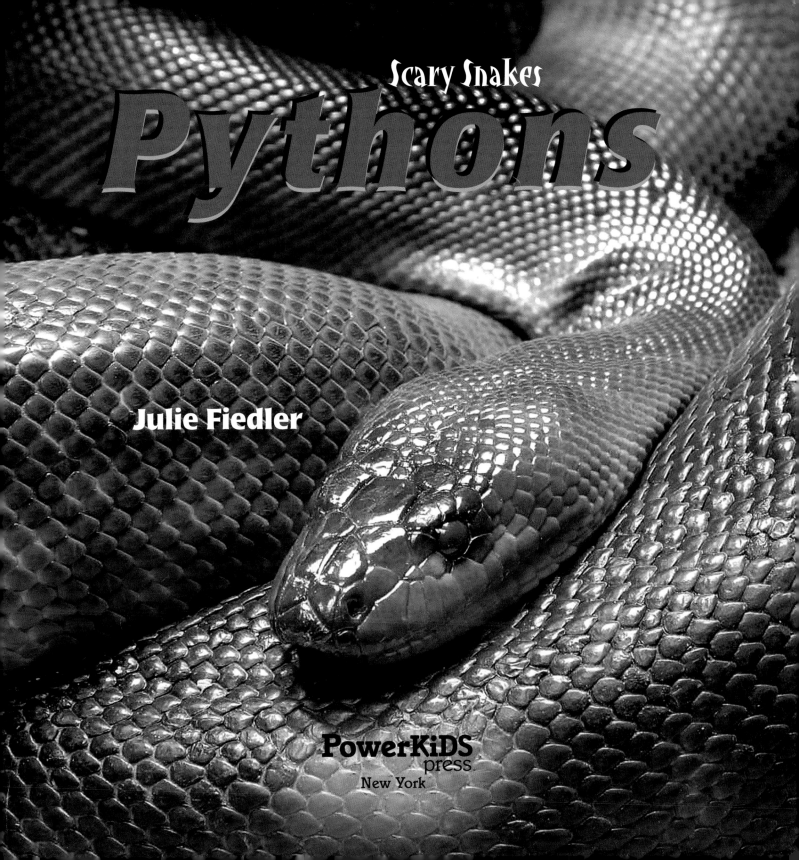

Scary Snakes

Pythons

Julie Fiedler

PowerKiDS press
New York

Published in 2008 by The Rosen Publishing Group, Inc.
29 East 21st Street, New York, NY 10010

First Edition

Editor: Jennifer Way
Book Design: Julio Gil
Layout Design: Kate Laczynski
Photo Researcher: Nicole Pristash

Photo Credits: Cover, pp. 1, 7, 11, 19 © Shutterstock.com; p. 5 © www.istockphoto.com/Yong Hian Lim; p. 9 © Fritz Polking/Peter Arnold, Inc.; pp. 13, 15, 21 © SuperStock, Inc.; p. 17 © AFP/Getty Images.

Library of Congress Cataloging-in-Publication Data

Fiedler, Julie.
  Pythons / Julie Fiedler. — 1st ed.
      p. cm. — (Scary snakes)
  Includes index.
  ISBN-13: 978-1-4042-3835-0 (library binding)
  ISBN-10: 1-4042-3835-2 (library binding)
  1. Pythons—Juvenile literature. I. Title.
  QL666.O67F54 2008
  597.96'78—dc22
                                        2007005439

Manufactured in the United States of America

Contents

What Are Pythons?

Pythons belong to a family, or group, of snakes called Pythonidae. They are some of the longest snakes in the world. They can be 3 to 33 feet (1–10 m) long and can weigh up to 300 pounds (136 kg)! The longest pythons have up to 400 sets of ribs.

Pythons are not **venomous**. This means they do not have a poisonous bite, as do vipers and pit vipers. Pythons are **dangerous** because they are **constrictors**.

This is a green tree python. This type of python lives in the rain forests of Australia and New Guinea.

5

Snakes That Squeeze

Pythons kill their **prey** by **squeezing** it to death. Pythons wrap around prey in a **coil**. Constriction does not squash bones. Pythons tighten their body so that the prey cannot breathe. Then they wait until the prey's heart stops. Pythons can feel when the prey is dead, and then they let go.

Scientists measured a python's squeeze at about 1 pound per square inch (.07 kg/sq cm). Pythons can kill animals as big as deer, crocodiles, and even people!

Pythons that live in trees, such as the Malaysian blood python, will coil around a branch loosely so they can rest. They coil and squeeze much harder when they need to kill prey.

Pythons on the Hunt

Pythons find prey by using their tongue and lips to sense the world around them. Their tongue senses gases in the air, and their lips sense heat.

Pythons hunt by **ambush**. Once they sense their prey, they hide until the prey comes near. Then pythons strike quickly. They use their teeth to hold the prey as they constrict. Pythons swallow their prey head first and eat it whole! They eat animals such as rats, pigs, and birds. Once pythons eat, they can go for a few days, weeks, or even years without eating again!

This rock python is in the middle of eating an impala. After the python is finished eating, it needs to stay still or else the impala might tear through its body!

Where Pythons Live

Pythons live in Australia, Africa, and Southeast Asia. They generally live in tropical, or warm, **climates** because they are cold blooded. That means they cannot control their body heat and so their climate must keep them warm.

Pythons live in rain forests, thick woods, and in areas with plenty of water, such as near rivers and lakes. Pythons are good at climbing and swimming. Some are **arboreal**, which means they live in trees. Others are **aquatic**, which means they live in water. Still other pythons live in holes in the ground.

Rain forest climates, like those found in Southeast Asia, can be home to pythons. *Inset:* This is a Malaysian blood python, which is found in the Southeast Asian country of Malaysia.

Snakes in Trees

Many pythons are **camouflaged**, which means they mix in with their **habitat**. Pythons that live in trees are different shades of green and brown. This helps them hide among the leaves and branches. Indian pythons live in tree hollows. Green tree pythons live in the top of trees.

Arboreal snakes are generally thinner than other snakes. That means they are lighter and can move around easily in the trees. They hang across branches. Some pythons are strong enough that they can hold on to branches as they hang down.

Arboreal pythons are often camouflaged to look like the leaves or branches among which they live. This is an Indian python.

13

Young Pythons

Female pythons lay eggs. They generally lay between 10 and 100 eggs at a time. When the females lay eggs, they place them in a pile and wrap their body around the eggs. The eggs can take two to three months to hatch, or open up.

When the females are coiled around the eggs, they make a trembling movement like a shiver with their body. This shiver is very unusual because it is one of the only times a snake can make its body warmer. This shiver helps the female keep the eggs warm.

The mother python's shivering is one of the few parental actions that are seen in any type of snake. If she is lucky, her eggs will hatch baby snakes, like the one shown here.

15

Burmese Pythons

Burmese pythons live in Burma, Malaysia, and Indonesia. They are one of the biggest snakes in the world. They can grow to be up to 25 feet (8 m) long and weigh up to 200 pounds (91 kg)! Female Burmese pythons usually grow to be larger than male Burmese pythons. Burmese pythons can live to be more than 20 years old.

Burmese pythons live in grassy habitats or in thick woods. They generally live near water and spend a lot of time swimming. They hunt at night and eat frogs, fish, birds, and small animals.

Pythons can make problematic pets and are best left alone in the wild or seen in zoos. This pet Burmese python is thought to have eaten a neighbor's cat!

Green Tree Pythons

Green tree pythons live in New Guinea and Australia. They live in rain forests. Green tree pythons are bright green, which helps keep them camouflaged in the trees and leaves. When they rest, they use their strong tail to hold on to tree branches. Then they make a coil with the rest of their body and rest their head in the middle of the coil.

Green tree pythons are about 6 to 8 feet (1.8–2.4 m) long. When their babies hatch, they are bright yellow or red. As they grow, they change color and finally become green when they are adults.

The green tree python's bright color helps it camouflage itself among the colorful leaves of its habitat.

Reticulated Pythons

Reticulated pythons are one of the longest snakes in the world. In fact, a reticulated python holds the record as the longest snake ever measured. It was more than 32 feet (10 m) long!

Reticulated pythons are usually gray, silver, or tan with colorful patterns along their back. Some reticulated pythons are albino, which means they are white and yellowish, with red eyes. Reticulated pythons can live over 30 years in **captivity**. They can be very dangerous and have killed people in the wild and in captivity.

Reticulated pythons live in the rain forests of Southeast Asia. These huge snakes can eat prey as large as a deer, horns and all!

Pythons and People

Even though pythons can kill people, people are also very dangerous to pythons! Many people hunt pythons to get their skin or eat their meat. Some types, such as the Indian python, are **endangered**.

Many people buy pythons to have as exotic pets. "Exotic" means "very unusual." Only people who have owned different snakes and exotic animals before should keep pythons as pets. Owners must be very careful when feeding pet pythons. Pythons might think the owner's hand is food and can attack it. Python attacks are more common in captivity than in the wild!

Glossary

ambush (AM-bush) An attack by surprise from a hiding place.

aquatic (uh-KWAH-tik) Living or growing in water.

arboreal (ahr-BOR-ee-ul) Having to do with trees.

camouflaged (KA-muh-flajhd) Hidden by looking like the things around one.

captivity (kap-TIH-vih-tee) A place where animals live, such as in a home, a zoo, or an aquarium, instead of living in the wild.

climates (KLY-mits) The kinds of weather certain areas have.

coil (KOYL) The ring or curl of something that is wound up.

constrictors (kun-STRIKT-urz) Snakes that kill by wrapping their body around their prey and squeezing.

dangerous (DAYN-jeh-rus) Might cause hurt.

endangered (in-DAYN-jerd) In danger of dying out.

habitat (HA-beh-tat) The kinds of land where an animal or a plant naturally lives.

prey (PRAY) An animal that is hunted by another animal for food.

squeezing (SKWEEZ-ing) Forcing together.

venomous (VEH-nuh-mis) Having a poisonous bite.

Index

C
coil, 6, 18

F
family, 4

H
habitat(s), 4, 16
heart, 6

I
Indian python, 12, 22

P
people, 6, 20, 22
pigs, 8
pit vipers, 4
prey, 6, 8
Pythonidae, 4

R
ribs, 4

T
teeth, 8
trees, 10, 12, 18

V
vipers, 4

Web Sites

Due to the changing nature of Internet links, PowerKids Press has developed an online list of Web sites related to the subject of this book. This site is updated regularly. Please use this link to access the list:

www.powerkidslinks.com/ssn/python/